D0430683

Delizioso!

 Panini the Italian Way

Carlo

PASCOE PUBLISHING, INC.
ROCKLIN, CALIFORNIA

©Pascoe Publishing, Inc., 2003

Cover design by Knockout Books

ISBN: 1-929862-30-X

Pascoe Publishing, Inc.
Rocklin, CA 95765
03 04 05 06 10 9 8 7 6 5 4 3 2 1

All books printed in Hong Kong

Table of Contents

Introduction

ITALY, the lush, rich country of inviting and intense culinary delights, invites you into the delightful world of grilled sandwiches called, "panini." For many years, Italians have been lining up at small cafés to enjoy panini for lunch or a snack. Because Italian businesses typically close between 11 a.m. and 2 p.m., customers can order an economical espresso and panini in the very casual café environment during those quiet hours. Whether a customer chooses a simple bread, cheese and olive oil panini or a heartier panini with smoked meats or seafood, the choices are usually varied and all are delectably delicious!

With the introduction of the De'Longhi Panini Maker, you now have the ability to create delicious grilled panini, bruschetta and crostini in your own home. "Panino," the Italian word for one sandwich, and "Panini" for more than one sandwich, start with a good, solid bread foundation. Select breads that are appropriate for grilling, such as rustic Italian breads, peasant breads, focaccia, and other breads that have a semi-solid texture. Bread slices should be between 1/4 inch to 1/2 inch in thickness for optimum results in the De'Longhi Panini Maker.

Panini are becoming popular for more than just a quick lunch. You will find recipes here that offer panini for breakfast, dinner and dessert, as well as a wide variety of choices for luncheon panini. Each recipe calls for ingredients that can be purchased in the specialty aisle of your grocery store or in specialty food and Italian import shops. The foods of Italy are truly a delight to enjoy and a warm grilled panini is the perfect way to sample that delight.

Buon Appetito!

Carlo

Panini— Spreads for Italian Grilling

Garlic Panini Spread

*This simple spread can be used as an accent for
just about any panini.*

1/2 CUP MAYONNAISE

1 TEASPOON GARLIC, CHOPPED

1 TABLESPOON FRESH ITALIAN PARSLEY, CHOPPED

Mix all ingredients in a small non-reactive container until well-blended. Store any unused spread in the refrigerator, tightly covered, for up to 2 weeks.

Makes 1/2 cup.

Salsa Rosa

The classic Italian red sauce used on panini and in salads.

3 TABLESPOONS MAYONNAISE

1 TEASPOON KETCHUP

2 TEASPOONS PREPARED TOMATO SAUCE

JUICE 1/2 LEMON

SALT AND PEPPER TO TASTE

Thoroughly blend all of the ingredients in a small, non-reactive container. Store any unused spread in the refrigerator, tightly covered, for up to 2 weeks.

Makes about 1/3 cup.

Honey Mustard Spread

*More American than Italian, the honey-mustard bite works
well with turkey and lean prosciutto or ham.*

1/2 CUP MAYONNAISE

1 TABLESPOON CLOVER HONEY

1 TABLESPOON PREPARED DIJON MUSTARD

Whisk or blend all of the ingredients in a small, non-reactive
bowl until well-combined. Cover tightly and chill until use. Store
any unused spread in the refrigerator for up to 2 weeks.

Makes 1/2 cup.

Fantastico Garlic Spread

*A garlic sauce guaranteed to delight garlic lovers.
Use this as a dip or spread for panini.*

16 CLOVES GARLIC, FINELY MINCED

1/2 TEASPOON SALT

1/4 CUP EXTRA VIRGIN OLIVE OIL

1/4 CUP FRESH LEMON JUICE

Place all of the ingredients in the blender or food processor
and pulse until the sauce is very smooth. Store any unused spread
in the refrigerator, tightly covered, for up to 2 weeks.

Makes about 1/2 cup.

Sun-Dried Tomato Spread

A lovely mélange of Italian flavors combine in this hearty spread. Use it on rustic breads or ciabatta for color and texture.

1/3 CUP SUN-DRIED TOMATOES PACKED IN OIL, DRAINED
AND SLICED

3 TABLESPOONS UNSALTED BUTTER, SOFTENED

1/4 CUP BLACK OLIVES, CHOPPED

SALT AND FRESHLY GROUND PEPPER TO TASTE

In a small bowl, blend the tomatoes, butter and olives together. Add salt and pepper to taste. Use immediately while the spread is softened. Store any unused spread in the refrigerator for up to 1 week.

Makes about 1/2 cup.

Zesty Zucchini Spread

Zucchini is an Italian favorite and this spread makes good use of the mild-flavored squash.

1 CUP ZUCCHINI, WELL-DRIED WITH ALL MOISTURE
  REMOVED, FINELY SHREDDED

1 CUP MOZZARELLA CHEESE, SHREDDED

1/2 CUP PIGNOLI NUTS, CHOPPED

1 TEASPOON LEMON JUICE

3/4 CUP MAYONNAISE

1 TABLESPOON GARLIC, CHOPPED

SALT AND PEPPER TO TASTE

Toss the zucchini and mozzarella together with a fork. Add the nuts and lemon juice. Add the mayonnaise, garlic, salt and pepper to taste and blend until all ingredients are combined. Store any unused spread in the refrigerator, tightly covered, for up to 1 week.

Makes about 2 1/2 cups spread.

Chickpea Garlic Spread

Borrowed from the Mediterranean, this spread is very similar to hummus. It can be used as a complement to panini and most roasted or raw vegetables.

1 CUP CANNED CHICKPEAS, DRAINED

1 TABLESPOON FRESH BASIL, CHOPPED

1 TABLESPOON FRESH OREGANO, CHOPPED

1 CLOVE GARLIC, MINCED

JUICE 1 LEMON

Place all of the ingredients in a blender or food processor and pulse until very smooth. Add a little bit of water to aid a smooth consistency while blending, if needed. Store in the refrigerator, tightly covered, for up to 2 weeks.

Anchovy, Olive and Caper Spread

The anchovies in this spread create an intense addition to any rustic bread.

4 OUNCES CANNED ANCHOVY FILLETS, DRAINED

1/4 CUP BLACK OLIVES, PITTED

2 TABLESPOONS CAPERS UNDER SALT, DRAINED AND
   WELL-RINSED

PINCH FRESHLY GROUND BLACK PEPPER

Place all ingredients in the blender or food processor and pulse until very smooth. Store any unused spread in the refrigerator, covered tightly, for up to 1 week.

Makes about 1/2 cup.

Classic Italian Pesto

Pesto is commonly used in Italy with pasta or vegetables, however it also makes a sturdy and flavorful spread for panini.

1 CUP FRESH BASIL, CLEANED AND ROUGHLY CHOPPED

1/4 CUP FRESH PARSLEY, CLEANED AND ROUGHLY CHOPPED

3 TABLESPOONS PARMESAN CHEESE, FRESHLY GRATED

3 CLOVES GARLIC, FINELY MINCED

3 TABLESPOONS PISTACHIO NUTS (OPTIONAL)

1/2 CUP HOT WATER

1/4 TEASPOON SALT

1/4 CUP EXTRA VIRGIN OLIVE OIL

Place the basil, parsley, cheese, garlic, nuts, hot water and salt in a blender or food processor. Pulse briefly to combine. While the blender or food processor is running at medium-high speed, pour a thin stream of oil into the herbs and mix until the pesto is very smooth. Store any unused pesto in the refrigerator, tightly covered, for up to 1 week.

Makes 1 1/2 cups.

Panini—
In the Tradition
of Italy

Bellissimo!

1 LARGE RED BELL PEPPER, CORED, SEEDED AND
    THINLY SLICED

1/2 SMALL RED ONION, PEELED AND THINLY SLICED

1 TEASPOON EXTRA VIRGIN OLIVE OIL

4 CIABATTA ROLLS, SPLIT

1/4 CUP GARLIC-INFUSED OLIVE OIL

SALT AND FRESHLY GROUND PEPPER TO TASTE

1/2 POUND PROSCIUTTO, THINLY SLICED

1/4 POUND PROVOLONE CHEESE, THINLY SLICED

1 C. ARUGULA, CLEANED AND CRISPED IN THE
    REFRIGERATOR

1 TABLESPOON EXTRA VIRGIN OLIVE OIL

In a small sauté pan over medium-high heat, sauté the red pepper and onion in the olive oil until the pepper is softened and the onion is translucent, about 3 to 4 minutes. Remove from the heat and place the vegetables in a small bowl.

To assemble the panini, place each of the rolls on a large working surface and open the rolls. Brush the cut side of each half with the garlic-infused olive oil and lightly salt and pepper. Layer on half of the rolls the prosciutto and provolone cheese. Layer on the remaining rolls the arugula leaves and the sautéed vegetables. Put the ciabatta together to form the panini. Lightly brush the outside of the panini with olive oil.

Grill the panini for 4 minutes in the panini maker on the medium setting, position one.

Makes 4 panini.

Lunch in the Vineyard

8 SLICES ITALIAN PEASANT BREAD, CUT INTO SLICES
    1/2-INCH THICK

1/4 CUP EXTRA VIRGIN OLIVE OIL

1 TABLESPOON ITALIAN RED WINE VINEGAR

PINCH SALT

1/4 TEASPOON FRESHLY GROUND BLACK PEPPER

8 OUNCE JAR MARINATED ARTICHOKE HEARTS, DRAINED

4 OUNCES GORGONZOLA CHEESE, CRUMBLED

2 CUPS ESCAROLE, WASHED AND DRAINED

2 TABLESPOONS EXTRA VIRGIN OLIVE OIL

Prepare the panini by placing the slices of bread on a flat working surface. Brush each slice with the olive oil and drizzle each with the Italian red wine vinegar. Dust each slice with the salt and pepper.

Place the artichoke hearts on a cutting board and flatten with the broad edge of a wide spatula or knife. Layer the artichoke hearts on 4 of the bread slices. Layer the Gorgonzola cheese over the artichoke hearts. On the remaining 4 slices of bread, arrange the escarole. Place the 4 remaining slices of bread over the layered slices and press together. Brush the outside of each panini with olive oil.

Grill the panini for 3 to 4 minutes in the panini maker on the medium setting, position one. Serve while warm.

Makes 4 panini.

·17·

Marco's Italian Cheese and Tomato Panini

4 SLICES PORTUGUESE BREAD

2 TABLESPOONS ANCHOVY, OLIVE & CAPER SPREAD
(SEE P. 12)

4 OUNCES SCAMORZA CHEESE, SLICED

2 GREEN TOMATOES, CLEANED AND DICED

2 ARTICHOKES, STEAMED

1 TABLESPOON EXTRA VIRGIN OLIVE OIL

Smooth the anchovy and olive spread over 2 slices of the Portuguese bread. Top with the scamorza and tomatoes. Remove the cooked artichoke hearts and mash with a fork. Lightly spoon equal portions of the artichokes over the layered pieces of bread. Place the 2 remaining slices of bread over the layered slices and lightly brush the outside of the panini with olive oil.

Grill in the panini maker for 3 to 4 minutes on the medium setting, position one.

Makes 2 panini.

Alessandro's Eggplant Panini

4 SLICES EGGPLANT, PEELED AND CUT INTO
    1/4-INCH THICK SLICES

2 TABLESPOONS EXTRA VIRGIN OLIVE OIL, DIVIDED

4 SLICES WHITE ITALIAN BREAD

2 TABLESPOONS GARLIC PANINI SPREAD (SEE P. 8)

1 TABLESPOON FRESH BASIL, CHOPPED

Lightly sauté the eggplant slices in 1 tablespoon of olive oil in a medium sauté pan. Cook until the eggplant is softened, about 4 minutes. Remove from the pan and set aside.

To assemble the panini, spread 2 slices of Italian bread with the garlic spread. Layer the eggplant slices over the spread. Top the eggplant with the basil. Cover the layered bread slices with the remaining bread slices and brush the outside of each panini with the remaining olive oil.

Grill in the panini maker for 3 to 4 minutes on the medium setting, position one.

Makes 2 panini.

The Piazza

4 SLICES ITALIAN-STYLE WHITE BREAD, SLICED THIN

2 TABLESPOONS SALSA ROSA* (SEE P. 8)

4 OUNCES PROSCIUTTO

4 THIN SLICES MOZZARELLA CHEESE

1 LARGE RIPE TOMATO, CORED AND SLICED THIN

1 TABLESPOON EXTRA VIRGIN OLIVE OIL

Place the slices of bread on a flat working surface. Spread a thin layer of salsa rosa on two pieces of the bread. Layer the prosciutto over the two pieces of bread. Place the mozzarella cheese over the prosciutto and add a layer of tomatoes over the cheese. Cover the layered slices of bread with the remaining two pieces of bread and lightly brush the outside of all of the slices with olive oil.

Grill in the panini maker for 3 to 4 minutes on the medium setting, position one.

*You may substitute drizzled olive oil on the bread slices in place of the Salsa Rosa.

Makes 2 panini.

Alpi (Alps)

4 SLICES RUSTIC WHOLE-GRAIN BREAD

1 TABLESPOON MAYONNAISE

4 OUNCES PROSCIUTTO, SLICED

4 THIN SLICES RED ONION

4 OUNCES BRIE CHEESE, CUT INTO SMALL PIECES

PINCH HOT RED PEPPER FLAKES

1 TABLESPOON EXTRA VIRGIN OLIVE OIL

Place the bread slices on a flat working surface. Evenly spread the mayonnaise on two slices of the bread. Layer the prosciutto, red onion and brie cheese over the two pieces of bread and add just a pinch of hot red pepper flakes. Cover the layered slices of bread with the remaining two pieces of bread and lightly brush the outside of all of the slices with olive oil.

Grill for 3-4 minutes in the panini maker on the medium setting, position one.

Makes 2 panini.

Toscana

4 SLICES CRUSTY ROSEMARY BREAD, SLICED THIN

1/4 C. SUN-DRIED TOMATO SPREAD (SEE P. 10)

4 OUNCES PROSCIUTTO, SLICED

1/4 CUP FRESH ARUGULA, CLEANED AND CRISPED IN THE REFRIGERATOR

4 THIN PIECES BRIE CHEESE

4 ROMA TOMATOES, CORED AND SLICED THIN

1 TABLESPOON EXTRA VIRGIN OLIVE OIL

Place the bread on a flat working surface. Lightly spread the sun-dried tomato spread on two pieces of bread. Layer slices of prosciutto over the spread and top with brie cheese and the Roma tomatoes. Arrange the arugula over the tomatoes. Cover the layered slices of bread with the remaining two pieces of bread and lightly brush the outside of all of the slices with olive oil.

Grill for 3-4 minutes in the panini maker on the medium setting, position one.

Makes 2 panini.

Tonno (Tuna)

2 4-INCH SQUARES OF FOCACCIA BREAD, SLICED IN HALF

1 TABLESPOON PREPARED TARTAR SAUCE

6 OUNCE CAN OIL-PACKED TUNA, DRAINED

4 ROMA TOMATOES, CORED AND SLICED

4 THIN PIECES BRIE CHEESE

4 LARGE ROMAINE LETTUCE LEAVES, CLEANED AND CRISPED
   IN THE REFRIGERATOR

1 TABLESPOON EXTRA VIRGIN OLIVE OIL

Place the focaccia bread on a flat working surface and spread the tartar sauce on two squares of the bread. Layer the tuna evenly over the sauce and top with the tomato slices and brie cheese. Cover with the romaine lettuce leaves. Cover the layered slices of bread with the remaining two pieces of bread. Lightly brush the outside of the focaccia slices with olive oil.

Grill for 2-3 minutes in the panini maker on the medium setting, position one.

Makes 2 panini.

Sierra

4 SLICES ROSEMARY BREAD, SLICED THIN

1 TABLESPOON SALSA ROSA (SEE P. 8)

4 OUNCES PROSCIUTTO, SLICED

4 THIN SLICES EDAM CHEESE

4 ROMA TOMATOES, CORED AND SLICED THIN

Place the slices of bread on a flat working surface. Evenly spread the salsa rosa over two pieces of the bread. Layer the prosciutto over the two slices and top with the tomato and edam cheese. Cover the layered slices of bread with the remaining two pieces of bread. Lightly brush the outside of the panini with olive oil.

Grill for 3-4 minutes in the panini maker on the medium setting, position one.

Makes 2 panini.

Marco's Arugula and Formaggio

2 FRENCH BAGUETTES, SLICED IN HALF HORIZONTALLY
(NO MORE THAN 1/2 INCH THICK)

4 TABLESPOONS EXTRA VIRGIN OLIVE OIL, DIVIDED

1/2 CUP ARUGULA, RINSED AND CRISPED IN THE REFRIGERATOR

4 THIN SLICES MOZZARELLA BUFALA CHEESE
(BUFFALO MOZZARELLA)

2 SMALL RED TOMATOES, CLEANED AND THINLY SLICED

SALT TO TASTE

Spread 2 of the sliced baguette pieces with 2 tablespoons of olive oil. Layer the arugula, mozzarella cheese and tomatoes over the olive oil. Season with salt to taste. Place the remaining 2 baguette halves over the layered halves and brush the outside of the panini with the remaining olive oil. Flatten the baguettes slightly by pressing down on them with your hand.

Grill for 4-5 minutes in the panini maker on the medium setting, position one.

Makes 2 panini.

Firenze (Florence)

2 4-INCH SQUARES OF FOCACCIA BREAD SLICED IN HALF

1 TABLESPOON SUN-DRIED TOMATO SPREAD (SEE P. 10)

4 ROMA TOMATOES, CORED AND SLICED THIN

1/2 RED ONION, PEELED AND SLICED THIN

1 TEASPOON GROUND OREGANO

4 OUNCES MOZZARELLA CHEESE, SLICED THIN

1 TABLESPOON EXTRA VIRGIN OLIVE OIL

Place the focaccia slices on a flat working surface. Cover two of the squares evenly with the sun-dried tomato spread. Layer the mozzarella cheese over the two slices and add the tomatoes and onion over the cheese. Dust each of the layered slices with the oregano. Cover the layered slices of focaccia with the remaining two pieces of focaccia. Lightly brush the outside of the panini with olive oil.

Grill for 3-4 minutes in the panini maker on the medium setting, position one.

Makes 2 panini.

Formaggi (cheese)

2 SMALL CRUSTY ROLLS

1 CLOVE GARLIC, PEELED AND CUT IN HALF

4 OUNCES BRIE CHEESE, CUT INTO 4 PIECES

4 OUNCES MOZZARELLA CHEESE, SLICED THIN

4 OUNCES EDAM CHEESE, SLICED THIN

1/2 CUP FRESH BABY SPINACH, BROKEN INTO SMALL PIECES

1 TABLESPOON EXTRA VIRGIN OLIVE OIL

Slice each roll in half. Rub the cut end of the garlic on each half of the rolls. Layer on two pieces of the rolls the brie cheese, mozzarella cheese and edam cheese. Top with the torn spinach. Place the remaining rolls on top of the layered rolls and lightly brush the outside of each roll with olive oil.

Grill for 3-4 minutes in the panini maker on the medium setting, position one.

Makes 2 panini.

Café Giuseppe

1/2 EGGPLANT, PEELED AND SLICED INTO PIECES
  1/2-INCH THICK

2 TABLESPOONS EXTRA VIRGIN OLIVE OIL, DIVIDED

4 SLICES ITALIAN STYLE WHITE BREAD, SLICED THIN

4 OUNCES SPECK (YOU MAY SUBSTITUTE PROSCIUTTO,
  IF DESIRED)

4 SLICES MOZZARELLA CHEESE

Place the eggplant in a colander and sprinkle the slices with salt. Place a heavy bowl on top of the eggplant and let the eggplant set for one hour. Rinse the eggplant and pat dry. Brush the eggplant with 1 tablespoon of the olive oil and arrange the slices on a baking sheet. Roast the slices in the oven at 400°F for 10 to 20 minutes, or until the eggplant is roasted and soft.

To assemble the panini, place the bread slices on a flat working surface. Layer two slices of the bread with the speck. Layer the mozzarella cheese and eggplant over the speck. Cover the layered slices of bread with the remaining two slices of bread. Lightly brush the outside of the panini with the remaining olive oil.

Grill for 2-3 minutes in the panini maker on the medium setting, position one.

Makes 2 panini.

Due Formaggi and Mushroom

2 4-INCH SQUARES OF ROSEMARY FOCACCIA BREAD
    SLICED IN HALF

1 TABLESPOON GARLIC, MINCED

1/2 CUP PREPARED MARINATED MUSHROOMS

4 OUNCES SOFT MOZZARELLA CHEESE, SLICED THIN

4 PIECES BRIE CHEESE

1 TABLESPOON EXTRA VIRGIN OLIVE OIL

Spread the minced garlic on two pieces of the focaccia bread. Layer over the garlic the marinated mushrooms, mozzarella cheese and brie cheese. Cover the layered squares of bread with the remaining two squares of bread. Lightly brush the outside of the panini with the olive oil.

Grill for 2-3 minutes in the panini maker on the medium setting, position one.

Makes 2 panini.

Carlo's Classico

1 EGGPLANT, PEELED AND SLICED INTO 1/4-INCH SLICES

1 SMALL ZUCCHINI, PEELED AND SLICED THIN

2 TABLESPOONS EXTRA VIRGIN OLIVE OIL

1 TABLESPOON GARLIC PANINI SPREAD (SEE P. 8)

4 SLICES CIABATTA BREAD, SLICED THIN

4 OUNCES PROSCIUTTO

2 SLICES EDAM CHEESE

1 TABLESPOON EXTRA VIRGIN OLIVE OIL

Place the eggplant slices in a colander and sprinkle the slices with salt. Place a heavy bowl on top of the eggplant and let the eggplant set for one hour. Rinse the eggplant and pat dry. Brush the eggplant slices and zucchini slices with 2 tablespoons of the olive oil and arrange the slices on a baking sheet. Bake the slices in the oven at 400°F for 10 to 20 minutes, or until the eggplant and zucchini are roasted and soft.

To assemble the panini, spread the garlic mayonnaise on 2 slices of the bread. Layer over the two slices the prosciutto, eggplant, zucchini and edam cheese. Cover the layered slices of bread with the remaining two slices of bread. Lightly brush the outside of the panini with the remaining olive oil.

Grill for 3-4 minutes in the panini maker on the medium setting, position one.

Makes 2 panini.

Pesce Panino

2 EGGS

SALT AND PEPPER TO TASTE

1/2 TEASPOON EXTRA VIRGIN OLIVE OIL

4 SLICES RUSTIC WHOLE-GRAIN BREAD

1 TABLESPOON MAYONNAISE

6 OUNCE CAN TUNA PACKED IN OIL, DRAINED

4 LEAVES ROMAINE LETTUCE, CLEANED AND CRISPED
IN THE REFRIGERATOR

1 TABLESPOON EXTRA VIRGIN OLIVE OIL

Beat the eggs in a medium mixing bowl and add salt and pepper to taste. Heat a small sauté pan and add the 1/2 teaspoon of olive oil. Add the eggs and swirl the eggs over the bottom of the pan. Allow the eggs to set omelet-style and remove from the pan.

Spread the mayonnaise on two slices of the bread. Divide the omelet in half and layer the omelet halves over the two slices of the bread. Scatter the tuna evenly over the eggs and place two pieces of romaine over each layered bread slice. Cover the layered slices of bread with the remaining two slices of bread. Lightly brush the outside of the panini with the olive oil.

Grill for 2-3 minutes in the panini maker on the low setting, position one.

Makes 2 panini.

Fabio's Special

2 4-INCH SQUARES OF FOCACCIA BREAD SLICED IN HALF

2 TABLESPOONS GARLIC PANINI SPREAD (SEE P. 8)

4 OUNCES PROSCIUTTO

4 OUNCES FONTINA CHEESE, THINLY SLICED

1 TABLESPOON BASIL, CHOPPED

1 TABLESPOON EXTRA VIRGIN OLIVE OIL

Spread the garlic mayonnaise on 2 squares of the focaccia. Layer over the mayonnaise the prosciutto and fontina cheese. Sprinkle the layered focaccia with the basil. Cover the layered slices of focaccia with the remaining two squares of focaccia. Lightly brush the outside of the panini with the olive oil.

Grill for 2-3 minutes in the panini maker on the medium setting, position one.

Makes 2 panini.

Calabrese

4 SLICES WHOLE-GRAIN BREAD

1 TABLESPOON MAYONNAISE

6 OUNCE CAN TUNA, PACKED IN OIL AND DRAINED

1 MEDIUM TOMATO, SLICED THIN

1/2 YELLOW ONION, PEELED AND SLICED THIN

1 TABLESPOON CAPERS, RINSED

1 TABLESPOON EXTRA VIRGIN OLIVE OIL

Spread two slices of the bread with mayonnaise. Layer the tuna, tomato and yellow onion over the 2 slices of the bread. Sprinkle the layered slices with the capers. Cover the layered slices of bread with the remaining 2 slices of bread. Lightly brush the outside of the panini with the olive oil.

Grill for 2-3 minutes in the panini maker on the medium setting, position one.

Makes 2 panini.

Buon Giorno

1 TEASPOON EXTRA VIRGIN OLIVE OIL

2 LARGE EGGS

4 SLICES WHITE ITALIAN BREAD

4 OUNCE JAR ROASTED RED PEPPERS, DRAINED AND CUT INTO SMALL PIECES

SALT AND PEPPER TO TASTE

1 TABLESPOON EXTRA VIRGIN OLIVE OIL

Heat 1 teaspoon of oil in a small sauté pan and add the eggs. Scramble the eggs over low heat until no moisture remains. Divide the eggs in half and place on 2 slices of the bread. Top the eggs evenly with the roasted red peppers. Sprinkle the layered slices with salt and pepper to taste. Cover the layered slices of bread with the remaining 2 slices of bread. Lightly brush the outside of the panini with the remaining olive oil.

Grill for 2-3 minutes in the panini maker on the medium setting, position one.

Makes 2 panini.

Panino Rustico

4 4-INCH SQUARES ROSEMARY FOCACCIA BREAD
4 OUNCE JAR ROASTED RED PEPPERS, CHOPPED
4 OUNCES PROVOLONE CHEESE, SLICED
1 TABLESPOON EXTRA VIRGIN OLIVE OIL

Spread the peppers evenly on 2 of the slices of bread. Layer the provolone cheese over the peppers and top with the remaining slices of bread. Brush the bread slices with the olive oil.

Grill for 2-3 minutes in the panini maker on the medium setting, position one.

Makes 2 panini.

Giardino

2 TABLESPOONS ZESTY ZUCCHINI SPREAD (SEE P. 11)
4 SLICES PEASANT-STYLE ITALIAN BREAD
1/2 CUP RED BELL PEPPER, SLICED
1/4 CUP RED ONION, THINLY SLICED
2 TABLESPOONS GARLIC, MINCED
1 TABLESPOON EXTRA VIRGIN OLIVE OIL

Cover 2 slices of the bread with the zucchini spread. Layer the pepper, onion and garlic over the zucchini spread. Cover the layered slices of bread with the remaining 2 slices of bread. Lightly brush the outside of the panini with the olive oil.

Grill for 2-3 minutes in the panini maker on the medium setting, position one.

Makes 2 panini.

Mamma's Favorite

1 SMALL EGGPLANT, PEELED AND CUT INTO 1/4-INCH SLICES

1 CUP ALL-PURPOSE FLOUR

2 EGGS

1 CUP ITALIAN-STYLE BREAD CRUMBS

2 TABLESPOONS VEGETABLE OIL

4 TABLESPOONS PREPARED MARINARA SAUCE

8 SLICES RUSTIC ITALIAN BREAD

4 OUNCES MOZZARELLA CHEESE, SLICED

1 TABLESPOON FRESH BASIL, CHOPPED

2 TABLESPOONS EXTRA VIRGIN OLIVE OIL

Layer the eggplant slices in a colander and sprinkle the slices with salt. Place a heavy dish on top of the eggplant and let stand for 1 hour. Rinse the eggplant slices and pat dry. Place the flour, egg and bread crumbs in separate shallow bowls. Dip each piece of eggplant into the flour, then the egg, followed by the bread crumbs. Heat a large frying pan to medium-high heat and add enough slices to cover the bottom of the pan. Fry the slices in batches in the vegetable oil until golden brown. Drain the eggplant slices on paper towels.

To assemble the panini, spread the marinara sauce equally on 4 slices of bread. Top the slices with eggplant slices and mozzarella cheese. Sprinkle the basil over the cheese. Cover the layered slices of bread with the remaining 4 slices of bread. Lightly brush the outside of the panini with the olive oil.

Grill 2 panini at a time for 3-4 minutes in the panini maker on the medium setting, position one.

Makes 2 panini.

Caroline's Special

1/2 POUND HOT OR SWEET ITALIAN SAUSAGES
(REMOVED FROM CASINGS)

1 GREEN BELL PEPPER, CORED AND SLICED THIN

1/2 YELLOW ONION, PEELED AND SLICED THIN

1/2 POUND RED POTATOES, SCRUBBED AND CUT INTO
SMALL CUBES

SALT AND PEPPER TO TASTE

4 SMALL CIABATTA ROLLS

1 TABLESPOON EXTRA VIRGIN OLIVE OIL

In a large sauté pan, brown the sausages over medium heat. Drain any grease and set the sausages aside. Sauté over medium heat the green bell pepper, yellow onion and potatoes until soft, about 8 minutes. Add the sausages and toss to combine the flavors together. Add salt and pepper to taste.

To assemble the panini, slice each roll in half. Layer 4 halves of the rolls evenly with the sausage, pepper, onion and potato mixture. Do not allow the sandwiches to become too thick. Cover the layered slices of ciabatta with the remaining 4 halves of ciabatta. Lightly brush the outside of the panini with the olive oil.

Grill 2 panini at a time for 4-5 minutes in the panini maker on the low setting, position one.

Makes 4 panini.

Famiglia Galante

2 BONELESS, SKINLESS CHICKEN BREAST HALVES

SALT AND PEPPER TO TASTE

4 SLICES WHITE ITALIAN BREAD

JUICE 1 LEMON

1 TABLESPOON FRESH BASIL, CHOPPED

6 OUNCE JAR MARINATED ARTICHOKE HEARTS
   (DRAINED AND SLICED THIN)

Pound out the 2 chicken breasts between 2 pieces of plastic wrap to a thickness of 1/4-inch each. Season the chicken with salt and pepper and grill in the panini maker on the low setting, position one for 5-7 minutes, or until the chicken is completely cooked and there is no pink remaining.

Place each chicken breast on 1 slice of bread. Squeeze the lemon juice over each chicken breast and top with the fresh basil. Evenly spread the artichoke hearts over the layered chicken panini. Cover the layered slices of bread with the remaining 2 slices of bread. Lightly brush the outside of the panini with the olive oil.

Grill for 2-3 minutes in the panini maker on the medium setting, position one.

Makes 2 panini.

The Sicilian

4 SLICES RUSTIC ITALIAN BREAD

1/4 POUND FRESH BABY SHRIMP, CLEANED AND COOKED, TAILS REMOVED

1 TABLESPOON SALSA ROSA SPREAD (SEE P. 8)

1/2 CUP ARUGULA, RINSED AND CRISPED IN THE REFRIGERATOR

1 TABLESPOON EXTRA VIRGIN OLIVE OIL

Spread the salsa rosa evenly over 2 pieces of the bread. Cover the slices with the baby shrimp and arugula. Cover the layered slices of bread with the remaining 2 slices of bread. Lightly brush the outside of the panini with olive oil.

Grill for 2-3 minutes in the panini maker on the medium setting, position one.

Makes 2 panini.

La Prima Colazione
Special

1/2 CUP PANCETTA, CHOPPED (YOU MAY SUBSTITUTE BACON,
 IF DESIRED)

1/2 CUP PORCINI MUSHROOMS, CLEANED AND SLICED

2 EGGS

1 TABLESPOON UNSALTED BUTTER

4 SLICES WHITE ITALIAN BREAD

4 OUNCES EDAM CHEESE

1 TABLESPOON EXTRA VIRGIN OLIVE OIL

In a large sauté pan, cook the pancetta over medium heat until slightly brown. Add the porcini mushrooms and cook until the mushrooms are soft. In a separate pan, scramble the eggs in the butter until just set. Add the eggs to the mushrooms and pancetta. Cook "omelet style" until eggs are firm.

To assemble, place half of the omelet on each of 2 pieces of bread. Top each omelet with half of the edam cheese. Cover the layered slices of bread with the remaining 2 slices of bread. Lightly brush the outside of the panini with olive oil.

Grill for 2-3 minutes in the panini maker on the medium setting, position one.

Makes 2 panini.

Vesuvio

4 SLICES WHITE ITALIAN BREAD

4 OUNCES GORGONZOLA CHEESE

4 OUNCES GENOA SALAMI, THINLY SLICED

2 TABLESPOONS EXTRA VIRGIN OLIVE OIL, DIVIDED

Spread the gorgonzola cheese on 2 slices of the bread. Cover the cheese with the salami slices and drizzle 1 tablespoon of olive oil over the salami. Cover the layered slices of bread with the remaining 2 slices of bread. Lightly brush the outside of the panini with olive oil.

Grill for 2 minutes in the panini maker on the medium setting, position one.

Makes 2 panini.

Mediterranean

2 TABLESPOONS EXTRA VIRGIN OLIVE OIL, DIVIDED

1 CUP PORCINI MUSHROOMS

2 BONELESS CHICKEN BREASTS, GRILLED AND CUT INTO
   BITE-SIZED PIECES

4 SLICES WHITE ITALIAN BREAD

4 OUNCES FONTINA CHEESE

1/2 CUP FRESH BABY SPINACH LEAVES

2 TABLESPOONS BALSAMIC VINEGAR

In a large sauté pan over medium heat, sauté the mushrooms in 1 tablespoon of the olive oil. Sauté the mushrooms until soft, about 3 minutes. Season the chicken with salt and pepper to taste and grill in the panini maker on the low setting, position one for 5-7 minutes, or until the chicken is completely cooked and no pink remains. Slice the chicken into bite-sized pieces and set aside.

To assemble the panini, divide the chicken evenly on 2 slices of the bread. Layer the mushrooms over the chicken and top with the fontina cheese and spinach leaves. Drizzle the balsamic vinegar over the layered bread and top with the remaining 2 slices of bread. Lightly brush the outside of the panini with olive oil.

Grill for 2-3 minutes in the panini maker on the medium setting, position one.

Makes 2 panini.

Nonna's Eggplant Panini

4 THIN SLICES EGGPLANT, PEELED AND SLICED
   1/4-INCH THICK

4 SLICES WHITE ITALIAN BREAD

2 TABLESPOONS CHICKPEA GARLIC SPREAD (SEE P. 12)

1/2 CUP ARUGULA, CLEANED AND CRISPED IN THE
   REFRIGERATOR

2 TABLESPOONS EXTRA VIRGIN OLIVE OIL, DIVIDED

Place the eggplant slices in a colander and sprinkle with salt. Arrange a heavy dish on top of the eggplant and let stand for 1 hour. Rinse the eggplant and pat dry.

Brush the eggplant with 1 tablespoon of olive oil. Grill the eggplant in the panini maker for 3-4 minutes on the low setting, position one.

To assemble the panini, spread the chickpea garlic spread on 2 slices of the bread. Top with the slices of the eggplant and arrange the arugula over the eggplant. Place the remaining 2 slices of bread over the layered bread and brush the outside of the panini with the remaining olive oil.

Grill for 2-3 minutes in the panini maker on the medium setting, position one.

Makes 2 panini.

Pizzaiola

2 TABLESPOONS PREPARED MARINARA SAUCE, DIVIDED

4 SLICES RUSTIC ITALIAN BREAD

1/4 POUND COOKED ROAST BEEF, SLICED THINLY

4 OUNCES FRESH MOZZARELLA CHEESE, SLICED

1 TABLESPOON FRESH ITALIAN PARSLEY, MINCED

FRESH BASIL AND OREGANO TO TASTE

1 TABLESPOON EXTRA VIRGIN OLIVE OIL

Spread 1 tablespoon of marinara sauce equally on two slices of bread. On the remaining 2 slices of bread layer the roast beef, mozzarella and parsley. Season with the basil and oregano to taste. Put the panini breads together and lightly brush the outside of the panini with olive oil.

Grill for 2-3 minutes in the panini maker on the medium setting, position one.

Makes 2 panini.

Portofino

6 OUNCES PORTOBELLO MUSHROOMS

2 TABLESPOONS EXTRA VIRGIN OLIVE OIL, DIVIDED

2 CIABATTA OR CRUSTY ROLLS, SLICED IN HALF

4 OUNCES PROVOLONE CHEESE, SLICED

1/2 CUP FRESH BABY SPINACH, CLEANED AND CRISPED IN
THE REFRIGERATOR

2 TABLESPOONS CLASSIC ITALIAN PESTO (SEE P. 13)

Lightly brush 1 tablespoon of olive oil on the portobello mushrooms. Grill the mushrooms for 3-4 minutes in the panini maker on the medium setting, position one.

To assemble, spread the pesto on 2 halves of the rolls. Top with the mushrooms, provolone cheese and the spinach leaves. Cover the layered rolls with the remaining halves of bread and lightly brush the outside of each panini with the remaining olive oil.

Grill for 3-4 minutes in the panini maker on the medium setting, position one.

Makes 2 panini.

Parma Panino

2 TABLESPOONS EXTRA VIRGIN OLIVE OIL, DIVIDED

1 TABLESPOON GARLIC, CHOPPED

1/4 CUP RED ONION, CHOPPED

4 SLICES WHITE ITALIAN BREAD

4 OUNCES PROSCIUTTO, SLICED

1/2 CUP FRESH BABY SPINACH LEAVES, CLEANED AND
CRISPED IN THE REFRIGERATOR

2 TABLESPOONS PARMESAN CHEESE

In a large sauté pan over medium heat, heat 1 tablespoon of the olive oil. When the oil is hot, add the garlic and onions and cook until the onions are soft and translucent. Add the spinach and sauté for another two minutes.

To assemble the panini, place the prosciutto over 2 slices of the bread and cover with the sautéed vegetables. Sprinkle with the Parmesan cheese and layer the spinach leaves over all. Place the remaining 2 slices of bread over the layered bread. Brush the outside of the panini with the remaining 1 tablespoon of oil.

Grill for 2-3 minutes in the panini maker on the medium setting, position one.

Makes 2 panini.

Molto Bene

1/2 CUP SALSA ROSA SPREAD (SEE P. 8)

8 PIECES 4-INCH SQUARE ROSEMARY FOCACCIA BREAD

8 OUNCES RICOTTA CHEESE

1 CUP FRESH SPINACH, COOKED AND FINELY CHOPPED
(YOU MAY SUBSTITUTE FROZEN, THAWED SPINACH,
IF DESIRED)

4 OUNCES MOZZARELLA CHEESE, SHREDDED

1 TABLESPOON PECORINO ROMANO CHEESE

1/4 CUP TOASTED PINE NUTS

1 TABLESPOON EXTRA VIRGIN OLIVE OIL

Evenly spread the salsa rosa on 4 squares of the focaccia bread. Blend together in a medium bowl, the ricotta cheese, spinach, mozzarella cheese, and Pecorino-Romano cheese. Layer the cheese and spinach spread evenly on 4 slices of bread. Scatter the toasted pine nuts over the layered focaccia. Place the remaining 2 squares of focaccia over the layered squares and brush the outside of the panini with olive oil.

Grill 2 panini at a time for 3-4 minutes in the panini maker on the medium setting, position one.

Makes 4 panini.

Buona Giornata!

4 TABLESPOONS EXTRA VIRGIN OLIVE OIL, DIVIDED

1 LARGE RED BELL PEPPER, CORED, SEEDED AND
    SLICED VERY THIN

1 LARGE GREEN BELL PEPPER, CORED, SEEDED AND
    SLICED VERY THIN

8 LARGE EGGS, BEATEN

8 PIECES 4-INCH SQUARE FOCACCIA BREAD, SLICED
    IN HALF HORIZONTALLY

2 TABLESPOONS BUTTER, MELTED

2 TABLESPOONS PARMESAN CHEESE, FRESHLY GRATED

Preheat 1 tablespoon of the olive oil in a large sauté pan over medium-high heat. Add the peppers, salt and pepper to taste and cook, turning frequently for approximately 20 minutes until lightly browned and tender. Pour the eggs over the peppers, cooking to allow the eggs to set. With a large spatula, turn once or twice to allow the eggs to set and cook until done.

Brush the melted butter on 4 pieces of the focaccia bread. Top each with peppers and eggs and sprinkle with Parmesan cheese. Place the remaining squares of focaccia over the layered squares and brush the outside of each panini with olive oil.

Grill for 2-3 minutes in the panini maker on the low setting, position one.

Makes 4 panini.

Fontina Saluti

2 SKINLESS, BONELESS CHICKEN BREAST HALVES,
POUNDED TO 1/4-INCH THICKNESS

2 TABLESPOONS EXTRA VIRGIN OLIVE OIL, DIVIDED

4 PIECES 4-INCH SQUARE FOCACCIA BREAD

3 TABLESPOONS CLASSIC ITALIAN PESTO (SEE P. 13)

4 OUNCES FONTINA CHEESE, SLICED

SALT AND PEPPER TO TASTE

Brush the chicken breast with 1 tablespoon of the olive oil and season with salt and pepper. Grill in the panini maker for approximately 5-7 minutes on the low setting, position one, until the chicken is completely cooked and no pink remains.

Spread the pesto sauce on 2 squares of the focaccia bread. Layer the chicken breasts and fontina cheese over the sauce. Place the 2 remaining pieces of focaccia over the layered pieces and brush the outside of the panini with the remaining olive oil.

Grill for 2-3 minutes in the panini maker on the medium setting, position one.

Makes 2 panini.

Chapter Tre

Panini—Italian with a Twist

Formaggi and Olive Pâté

4 SLICES ITALIAN STYLE WHITE BREAD, THINLY SLICED

2 TABLESPOONS PREPARED OLIVE PÂTÉ

4 OUNCES SPECK (YOU MAY SUBSTITUTE PROSCIUTTO,
IF DESIRED)

4 PIECES BRIE CHEESE

1 TABLESPOON EXTRA VIRGIN OLIVE OIL

Place the bread slices on a flat working surface. Spread the olive pâté on two slices of the bread. Layer the speck evenly on the two slices and top with the brie cheese. Cover the layered slices of bread with the remaining two slices of bread. Lightly brush the outside of the panini with the remaining olive oil.

Grill for 2-3 minutes in the panini maker on the medium setting, position one.

Makes 2 panini.

Pacific Northwest

1 TABLESPOON GARLIC PANINI SPREAD (SEE P. 8)

4 SLICES PEASANT-STYLE ITALIAN BREAD

1 TABLESPOON CAPERS, RINSED

1/2 YELLOW ONION, PEELED AND FINELY CHOPPED

4 OUNCES SMOKED SALMON

1 TABLESPOON EXTRA VIRGIN OLIVE OIL

Spread the garlic mayonnaise on 2 slices of the bread. Layer the slices with the capers and onions. Spread the salmon overall. Cover the layered slices of bread with the remaining 2 slices of bread. Lightly brush the outside of the panini with the olive oil.

Grill for 2-3 minutes in the panini maker on the medium setting, position one.

Makes 2 panini.

Walter's Canadian Bacon and Parmesan Panini

4 SLICES 12-SEED BREAD

3 TABLESPOONS EXTRA VIRGIN OLIVE OIL

4 SLICES CANADIAN BACON, SLIGHTLY GRILLED
(YOU MAY SUBSTITUTE VEGETARIAN CANADIAN
BACON, IF DESIRED)

4 SLICES SWISS CHEESE

2 GREEN OLIVES, PITTED AND SLICED

DASH PREPARED YELLOW MUSTARD

Lightly brush 2 slices of the bread with olive oil. Layer the Canadian bacon, cheese and green olives over the slices. On the remaining 2 slices of bread, thinly spread a bit of prepared mustard. Put the panini together and lightly brush the outside of each with the remaining olive oil.

Grill for 3-4 minutes in the panini maker on the medium setting, position one.

Makes 2 panini.

Americano

2 TABLESPOONS EXTRA VIRGIN OLIVE OIL

1 CLOVE GARLIC, CHOPPED

1 SMALL YELLOW ONION, PEELED AND CHOPPED

1/2 POUND WHITE BUTTON MUSHROOMS,
CLEANED AND SLICED

1/2 POUND GROUND BEEF

4 SLICES ROMAINE LETTUCE

4 OUNCES MOZZARELLA CHEESE, SLICED THIN

4 CIABATTA ROLLS, CUT IN HALF

SALT AND PEPPER TO TASTE

2 TABLESPOONS EXTRA VIRGIN OLIVE OIL

Lightly sauté the garlic, onion and mushrooms in 2 table-spoons of olive oil over medium-low heat until the vegetables are tender. Remove the vegetables from the pan. Add the ground beef to the sauté pan and cook over medium-high heat until browned. Crumble the beef as it cooks. Drain any grease from the beef and replace the vegetables to the pan. Combine the beef with the vegetables, tossing lightly, and season with the salt and pepper. Stir just until blended.

To assemble the panini, layer the romaine lettuce, ground beef and slices of mozzarella cheese on 4 halves of the ciabatta. Cover the layered slices of ciabatta with the remaining 4 halves of ciabatta. Lightly brush the outside of the panini with the olive oil.

Grill for 3-4 minutes in the panini maker on the medium setting, position one.

Makes 4 panini.

Italian PB and J

4 SLICES WHITE ITALIAN BREAD

2 TABLESPOONS NUTELLA® SPREAD

1 MEDIUM RIPE BANANA, PEELED AND THINLY SLICED

2 TABLESPOONS UNSALTED BUTTER, MELTED

Spread 1 tablespoon of Nutella on 2 slices of the bread. Cover the Nutella evenly with the banana slices. Cover the layered slices of bread with the remaining 2 slices of bread. Lightly brush the outside of the panini with the butter.

Grill for 2-3 minutes in the panini maker on the low setting, position one.

Makes 2 panini.

Francesco's Prosciutto and Smoked Scamorza Panini

2 PIECES POCKETLESS PITA BREAD

2 SLICES PRAGUE PROSCIUTTO (YOU MAY SUBSTITUTE
   OTHER TYPES OF IMPORTED PROSCIUTTO,
   IF DESIRED)

4 SLICES SMOKED SCAMORZA CHEESE

2 TABLESPOONS SUN-DRIED TOMATOES IN OIL

SPLASH MILD OIL-BALSAMIC VINAIGRETTE

1 TABLESPOON EXTRA VIRGIN OLIVE OIL

Layer on one-half of each pita, the prosciutto, scamorza cheese and sundried tomatoes. Splash a bit of the vinaigrette over all and fold the pita over to cover all. Lightly brush the outside of each panini with olive oil.

Grill for 3-4 minutes in the panini maker on the medium setting, position one.

Makes 2 panini.

Sweet Italian Toast

2 EGGS

1 TABLESPOON GRANULATED SUGAR

4 SLICES PANNETONE

2 TABLESPOONS NUTELLA® SPREAD

2 TABLESPOONS UNSALTED BUTTER, MELTED

POWDERED SUGAR FOR GARNISH

In a large bowl, mix together the eggs and granulated sugar. Dip each slice of the pannetone into the egg mixture, evenly coating all sides of the pannetone. Spread the Nutella on 2 slices of pannetone. Place the remaining 2 slices of pannetone over the coated slices and lightly brush the outside of the panini with the melted butter.

Grill for 2-3 minutes in the panini maker on the medium setting, position one. Sprinkle with powdered sugar to garnish.

Makes 2 panini.

Polenta Pomodoro

1 POUND TUBE PREPARED POLENTA

2 TABLESPOONS EXTRA VIRGIN OLIVE OIL

SALT AND PEPPER TO TASTE

4 OUNCES SOFT MOZZARELLA CHEESE, THINLY SLICED

1 ROMA TOMATO, CORED AND DICED

Cut the prepared polenta into slices 1/4-inch thick. Brush each slice with olive oil and sprinkle with salt and pepper to taste.

Grill the polenta slices for 5 minutes on the high setting, position one until crispy and golden. Serve hot, topped with a thin slice of soft mozzarella, 1 teaspoon of chopped tomato and a drizzle of extra virgin olive oil.

Serves 6.

O Sole Mio

2 LARGE PORTOBELLO MUSHROOMS, CLEANED

3 TABLESPOONS EXTRA VIRGIN OLIVE OIL, DIVIDED

2 CLOVES GARLIC, MINCED

4 TABLESPOONS PREPARED PESTO

8 PIECES 4-INCH SQUARE FOCACCIA BREAD, SLICED IN HALF

1 CUP FRESH BABY SPINACH LEAVES, CLEANED AND CRISPED
   IN THE REFRIGERATOR

4 OUNCES MOZZARELLA CHEESE, SLICED THIN

Preheat the oven to 400 degrees. Trim the mushroom stems and cut into slices 1/4-inch thick. Brush 1 tablespoon of the olive oil on both sides of each mushroom and place the mushrooms in the broiler pan. Sprinkle each mushroom lightly with the garlic. Broil the mushrooms until tender, about 10 minutes, turning once.

Spread pesto on 4 slices of the bread. Layer the mushrooms and spinach over the prepared bread and top with the mozzarella cheese. Place the remaining focaccia over the layered focaccia and brush the outside of the panini lightly with the remaining oil.

Grill for 3-4 minutes in the panini maker on the medium setting, position one.

Makes 4 panini.

Deutschland

4 SLICES ITALIAN STYLE WHITE BREAD, SLICED THIN

1 TABLESPOON PREPARED YELLOW MUSTARD

2 FRANKFURTERS OR POLISH SAUSAGES, SLICED
THIN HORIZONTALLY

1/2 CUP CANNED SAUERKRAUT, DRAINED

Place the bread slices on a flat working surface. Spread the mustard evenly on two slices of the bread. Layer the two slices with the hot dog slices and the sauerkraut. Cover the layered slices of bread with the remaining two slices of bread. Lightly brush the outside of the panini with olive oil.

Grill for 5-6 minutes in the panini maker on the low setting, position one.

Makes 2 panini.

New York Deli Panini

4 SLICES WHOLE GRAIN BREAD

1 TABLESPOON GRAINY MUSTARD

1 TABLESPOON MAYONNAISE

1/4 POUND DELI SMOKED HAM, SLICED THIN

1/4 POUND SMOKED PROVOLONE CHEESE, SLICED THIN

1 TABLESPOON EXTRA VIRGIN OLIVE OIL

Spread the mustard and mayonnaise evenly on 2 slices of the bread. Top each of the slices with the ham and provolone cheese. Place the remaining slices of bread over the layered slices and lightly brush the outside of the panini with olive oil.

Grill 2-3 minutes in the panini maker on the medium setting, position one.

Makes 2 panini.

Crostini and Bruschetta the Italian Way

Classica Bruschetta

1 LOAF ITALIAN RUSTIC OR CIABATTA BREAD

1 CLOVE GARLIC, PEELED

3 TABLESPOONS EXTRA VIRGIN OLIVE OIL

Slice the bread diagonally into pieces 1/2-inch thick. Rub the garlic clove over each slice. Brush each slice with the olive oil. Grill the bruschetta in the panini maker for 2-3 minutes on the medium setting, position one.

Makes 8 to 12 bruschetta.

Tuscany Bruschetta

1 LOAF ITALIAN RUSTIC OR CIABATTA BREAD

3 TABLESPOONS EXTRA VIRGIN OLIVE OIL

2 ROMA TOMATOES, CORED, SEEDED, AND DICED

2 CLOVES GARLIC, MINCED

1 TEASPOON BALSAMIC VINEGAR

1 TABLESPOON FRESH BASIL, MINCED

Slice the bread diagonally into pieces 1/2-inch thick. Brush each slice with the olive oil. Grill the bruschetta in the panini maker for 2-3 minutes on the medium setting, position one.

Layer the tomatoes and garlic over each grilled bruschetta and drizzle the balsamic vinegar and basil over all.

Makes 8 to 12 bruschetta.

Piccolo Pepper
Bruschetta

1 LOAF TALIAN RUSTIC OR CIABATTA BREAD

4 TABLESPOONS EXTRA VIRGIN OLIVE OIL

2 CLOVES GARLIC, MINCED

4 OUNCE JAR ROASTED RED PEPPERS, DRAINED

2 TABLESPOONS PARMESAN CHEESE, GRATED

Slice the bread diagonally into pieces 1/2-inch thick. Use 3 tablespoons of olive oil to brush the slices on both sides. Grill the bruschetta in the panini maker for 2-3 minutes on the medium setting, position one.

Scatter the garlic over the bruschetta. Thinly slice the red peppers and layer them over the bruschetta. Sprinkle each bruschetta with the grated parmesan cheese. Lightly drizzle each bruschetta with the remaining olive oil.

Makes 8 to 12 bruschetta.

Pinoli and Pesto Bruschetta

1 LOAF ITALIAN RUSTIC OR CIABATTA BREAD

4 TABLESPOONS EXTRA VIRGIN OLIVE OIL, DIVIDED

1/2 CUP CLASSIC ITALIAN PESTO (SEE P. 13)

1/2 CUP TOASTED PINOLI (PINE NUTS)

Slice the bread diagonally into pieces 1/2-inch thick. Use 3 tablespoons of olive oil to brush the slices on both sides. Grill the bruschetta in the panini maker for 2-3 minutes on the medium setting, position one.

Spread a thin layer of pesto on each piece of bruschetta. Sprinkle the toasted pine nuts over the pesto and lightly drizzle with the remaining olive oil.

Makes 8 to 12 bruschetta.

Delizie!

1 LOAF ITALIAN RUSTIC OR CIABATTA BREAD

4 TABLESPOONS EXTRA VIRGIN OLIVE OIL, DIVIDED

1 CLOVE GARLIC, MINCED

4 OUNCES FRESH MOZZARELLA CHEESE, SLICED THIN

2 ROMA TOMATOES CORED, SEEDED, AND DICED

1 TABLESPOON FRESH OREGANO, CHOPPED

1 TABLESPOON FRESH BASIL, CHOPPED

Slice the bread diagonally into pieces 1/2-inch thick. Use 3 tablespoons of olive oil to brush the slices on both sides. Grill the bruschetta in the panini maker for 2-3 minutes on the medium setting, position one.

Layer each bruschetta with the garlic, mozzarella, diced tomatoes, oregano and basil. Drizzle the bruschetta lightly with the remaining olive oil.

Makes 8 to 12 bruschetta.

Buon Appetito!

1 LOAF ITALIAN RUSTIC OR CIABATTA BREAD

4 TABLESPOONS EXTRA VIRGIN OLIVE OIL, DIVIDED

4 OUNCES FRESH MOZZARELLA CHEESE, SLICED

6 OUNCE CAN TUNA PACKED IN OIL, DRAINED

1 SMALL YELLOW OR RED ONION, CHOPPED

2 ROMA TOMATOES, CORED, SEEDED AND DICED

Slice the bread diagonally into pieces 1/2-inch thick. Use 3 tablespoons of olive oil to brush the slices on both sides. Grill the bruschetta in the panini maker for 2-3 minutes on the medium setting, position one.

Top each bruschetta with the sliced mozzarella. In a small mixing bowl, combine the tuna with the chopped onions and layer the mixture over the mozzarella. Spoon the diced tomatoes over all and add a drizzle of the remaining olive oil on each bruschetta.

Makes 8 to 12 bruschetta.

Shrimp and Basil Bruschetta

1 LOAF ITALIAN RUSTIC OR CIABATTA BREAD

4 TABLESPOONS EXTRA VIRGIN OLIVE OIL, DIVIDED

1 TABLESPOON GARLIC, MINCED

1/4 POUND SMALL UNCOOKED SHRIMP, CLEANED AND
DEVEINED, TAILS REMOVED

JUICE 1/2 LEMON

1 TABLESPOON FRESH BASIL, CHOPPED

Slice the bread diagonally into pieces 1/2-inch thick. Use 3 tablespoons of olive oil to brush the slices on both sides. Grill the bruschetta in the panini maker for 2-3 minutes on the medium setting, position one.

In a small sauté pan, cook the garlic over medium heat in the remaining olive oil until the garlic is softened. Add the shrimp and continue cooking until the shrimp are pink and opaque throughout. Spoon the shrimp and garlic over each slice of bruschetta and sprinkle each lightly with lemon juice. Garnish with the fresh basil over all.

Makes 8 to 12 bruschetta.

Lamponi (Raspberry) Dessert Bruschetta

1 LOAF ITALIAN RUSTIC OR CIABATTA BREAD

4 TABLESPOONS UNSALTED BUTTER, DIVIDED

2 CUPS FRESH RASPBERRIES, CLEANED AND CUT INTO
   SMALL PIECES

2 TABLESPOONS AMARETTO LIQUEUR

2 TABLESPOONS POWDERED SUGAR

1/4 CUP TOASTED ALMONDS, SLIVERED

Slice the bread diagonally into pieces 1/2-inch thick. Use 3 tablespoons of butter to brush the slices of bread on both sides. Grill the bruschetta in the panini maker for 2-3 minutes on the medium setting, position one. Cool completely.

In a medium mixing bowl, combine the raspberries and Amaretto. Cover and allow the flavors to marry in the refrigerator for 1 hour. Top each bruschetta with the berries and sprinkle each with powdered sugar. Use the toasted almonds as a garnish for each bruschetta.

Espresso and Mascarpone Dessert Bruschetta

1 LOAF ITALIAN RUSTIC OR CIABATTA BREAD

4 TABLESPOONS UNSALTED BUTTER, DIVIDED

1 CUP MASCARPONE CHEESE

2 TABLESPOONS MARSALA WINE

2 TABLESPOONS ESPRESSO COFFEE

2 TABLESPOONS GRANULATED SUGAR

1 TEASPOON PURE VANILLA EXTRACT

2 TABLESPOONS MINI SEMI-SWEET CHOCOLATE CHIPS

Slice the bread diagonally into pieces 1/2-inch thick. Use 3 tablespoons of butter to brush the slices of bread on both sides. Grill the bruschetta in the panini maker for 2-3 minutes on the medium setting, position one. Cool completely.

In a medium bowl, combine the mascarpone cheese with the marsala wine. Blend well and add the espresso, sugar and the vanilla extract until smooth. Spread the cheese and espresso mixture on each bruschetta and sprinkle with the chocolate chips.

Makes 8 to 12 bruschetta.

Fragole (Strawberry)
Dessert Bruschetta

1 LOAF ITALIAN RUSTIC OR CIABATTA BREAD

4 TABLESPOONS UNSALTED BUTTER, DIVIDED

1 CUP MASCARPONE CHEESE

1/4 CUP POWDERED SUGAR

1 CUP STRAWBERRIES, CLEANED AND CUT INTO
   SMALL PIECES

1 TEASPOON GROUND CINNAMON.

Slice the bread diagonally into pieces 1/2-inch thick. Use 3 tablespoons of butter to brush the slices of bread on both sides. Grill the bruschetta in the panini maker for 2-3 minutes on the medium setting, position one. Cool completely.

In a small bowl, blend the mascarpone and sugar until smooth. Lightly fold in the strawberries. Spread the cheese and strawberries on each bruschetta and sprinkle lightly with cinnamon.

Makes 8 to 12 bruschetta.

Almond and Peach Dessert Bruschetta

1 LOAF ITALIAN RUSTIC OR CIABATTA BREAD

4 TABLESPOONS UNSALTED BUTTER, DIVIDED

1 CUP MASCARPONE CHEESE

1 CUP FRESH PEACHES, PEELED, PITTED AND CUT INTO BITE SIZED PIECES

2 TABLESPOONS AMARETTO LIQUEUR

1/4 CUP GRANULATED SUGAR

2 TABLESPOONS TOASTED ALMONDS, SLIVERED

Slice the bread diagonally into pieces 1/2-inch thick. Use 3 tablespoons of butter to brush the slices of bread on both sides. Grill the bruschetta in the panini maker for 2-3 minutes on the medium setting, position one. Cool completely.

In a small mixing bowl, blend the mascarpone cheese with the Amaretto and sugar until smooth. Spread the cheese mixture on each bruschetta. Top with the peaches and sprinkle with slivered almonds.

Makes 8 to 12 bruschetta.

Eugenio's Milano Crostini

4 SLICES RUSTIC ITALIAN BREAD, ABOUT 1/4-INCH THICK

1 TABLESPOON EXTRA VIRGIN OLIVE OIL

1 SMALL CUCUMBER, PEELED, SEEDED, AND SLICED THIN

1/2 CUP CARROTS, SHREDDED

4 OUNCES CAPRINO CHEESE (YOU MAY SUBSTITUTE
GOAT CHEESE, IF DESIRED)

Brush each slice of bread with the olive oil and grill each slice in the panini maker for 2-3 minutes on the medium setting, position one.

Layer the crostini with the cucumbers and shredded carrots. Top each crostini with the caprino cheese.

Serves 4.

Black Olive Crostini

4 SLICES RUSTIC ITALIAN BREAD, ABOUT 1/4-INCH THICK

2 TABLESPOONS EXTRA VIRGIN OLIVE OIL, DIVIDED

1/2 CUP RIPE BLACK OLIVES, PITTED

1 CLOVE GARLIC, MINCED

1 TEASPOON LEMON JUICE

1 TEASPOON FRESH PARSLEY, MINCED

1/2 TEASPOON DIJON MUSTARD

Lightly brush 1 tablespoon of the olive oil over the slices of the bread. Grill each slice in the panini maker for 2-3 minutes on the medium setting, position one.

Place all of the remaining ingredients in a blender or food processor and pulse until partially smooth. Top each of the crostini with the olive spread.

Makes 4 crostini.

Chapter Cinque

Glossary

Anchovies: *(Acciughe)*

Anchovies are small canned fish and are preserved under oil or salt. If salted, they should be well-rinsed before use. Anchovies offer excellent flavor for Italian sauces and spreads and can typically be found near the tuna in the grocery store.

Balsamic Vinegar: *(Aceto Balsamico)*

Balsamic vinegar is the intense and flavorful vinegar that comes from Modena, Italy. The best brands are aged for 10 years in casks made of aromatic woods. The intensity of this vinegar requires only a few drops for flavoring spreads, pastas, salads, meats and poultry. Look for balsamic vinegar in the specialty aisle of your grocery store.

Basil: *(basilico)*

The backbone of Italian pesto, basil is a savory herb that graces many Italian foods. Use it fresh for best results.

Bruschetta: *(Bruschetta)*

A small piece of bread that is brushed with olive oil or butter and is toasted or grilled. Bruschetta breads are typically 1/2 inch thick and are topped with tomatoes, garlic, parsley or any other number of toppings.

Ciabatta: *(Ciabatta)*

Firm Italian bread rolls that are round or oval in shape. Ciabatta are perfect partners for panini because they are not too thick and have a firm texture for layering ingredients.

Crostini: *(Crostini)*

Crostini are similar to bruschetta in that they are grilled with olive oil or butter. They are not as thick as bruschetta breads and are typically used with lighter fare as toppings or no toppings at all.

Extra Virgin Olive Oil: *(Extra Vergine di Oliva)*

Extra virgin olive oil is the result of the first cold pressing of olives. Either filtered or unfiltered, it is best when it is light and contains less than 1% acidity (extra virgin). Oil will break down with heat so it should not be used for deep frying or other high heat methods of food preparation and should be stored in a cool, dark place. Store the oil in a glass, glazed clay or stainless steel container. Do not store oil in an iron, copper or plastic container. Olive oils that have a greater than 1% acidity level are:

1 – 1.5% fine virgin

1.5 – 3% regular virgin

3 – 4% pure (or virgin)

There are many distinctions to the variety and qualities of olive oil. Colors may vary from yellow to deep green (depending on when the olives were harvested and the type of olives pressed) and your favorite oils may be found simply by testing the ones that look the most appealing to you.

Focaccia: *(Focaccia)*

A thick Italian bread topped with herbs, spices, garlic, onions, tomatoes or other flavorings. Focaccia is usually cut into squares for serving.

Gorgonzola cheese: *(gorgonzola)*

Gorgonzola from Northern Italy is a creamy member of the blue cheese family and can be identified by its bite and intense cheese flavor. Use it crumbled or softened in any variety of Italian recipes for extra flavor.

Mascarpone *(Mascarpone)*

A very smooth and dense cream cheese made in Italy. Perfect when paired with any dessert recipe.

Panini: *(Panino; Panini)*

In Italian, "panino" (singular) and "panini" (plural) are interchangeable for the English word, "sandwich." Customarily, panini can be grilled or not, however the most popular method is to grill the sandwiches with fillings of meat, fish, cheese, herbs and oil.

Parmesan: *(Reggiano Parmigiano)*

Parmesan is a favorite cheese for almost any Italian dish. A good brand of Parmesan cheese is aged for at least 12 months or more. Grate the Parmesan just before using for best results.

Pine Nuts: *(Pinoli; Pine Kernels)*

Kernels of the pine tree, pine nuts are used extensively in pesto and as a garnish for many popular Italian dishes.

Prosciutto: *(prosciutto di Parma; prosciutto cotto)*

Prosciutto (Italian baked ham or bacon) is typically served in very thin strips and has a deep red color and a high degree of marbled fat throughout. You may substitute bacon or very thin slices of ham, if desired, but for the best results, choose a high quality prosciutto imported from Italy.

Rosemary: *(Rosmarino)*

Rosemary is an aromatic herb that is widely used in Italy. Use fresh rosemary when possible and dried rosemary as a second choice.

Scamorza: *(Scamorza)*

This cheese is firm and especially tasty when smoked. You may substitute any other smoked cheese that has a solid texture.

Speck: *(speck)*

Speck is sliced thinly and used often used in Italian panini. It is typically smoked and is very similar to smoked ham.